Sovereign God loves in
His Everlasting way!
He'll never fail you!

Joshua!
Per Carltele

PRAY SIMPLY

AND

SIMPLY PRAY

ENDORSEMENTS

Marie Miller is a woman of God and has shown through her years of ministry as a pastor and evangelist her understanding of the simplicity of prayer. We often complicate prayer unnecessarily. God simply invites us to enter into a living relationship with Him in which prayer is at the core, for it is through *simply praying*—conversing with God and listening to His responses—that we become acquainted with His ways of thinking and doing. God tells us that His ways are not our ways and His thoughts are not our thoughts, but as the heavens are higher than the earth so are His ways higher than our ways and His thoughts than our thoughts (Isaiah 55:8-9). *Pray Simply—Simply Pray* is a book that will help you into a place in your relationship with God where you will increasingly understand the mind and heart of God for you and the world you live in.

Reverend Harold Reid
The Pentecostal Assemblies of Canada

There surely cannot be a more important subject about which to teach the Body of Christ, than this privilege of communication with God through prayer. Marie Miller, incorporating her extensive knowledge of the Word of God and her own personal experiences, brings to light what is necessary for us to learn how to break through potential prayer barriers and launch into intercession that can transform our personal lives and circumstances as well as the world around us. *Pray Simply—Simply Pray* is a valuable resource and a must-read for both new and established believers.

Kathy Bousquet
PAOC Missions Prayer Facilitator

PRAY SIMPLY AND
SIMPLY PRAY

 CASTLE QUAY BOOKS

PRAY SIMPLY AND SIMPLY PRAY

Copyright © 2011 Marie A Miller
All rights reserved
Printed in Canada
International Standard Book Number: 978-1-894860-46-8

Published by:
Castle Quay Books
1307 Wharf Street, Pickering, Ontario, L1W 1A5
Tel: (416) 573-3249
E-mail: info@castlequaybooks.com
www.castlequaybooks.com

Cover design by Essence Graphic Design
Printed at Essence Printing, Belleville, Ontario

Library and Archives Canada Cataloguing in Publication

Miller, Marie A., 1961-

    Pray simply, simply pray : you can do it! / Marie A. Miller.

ISBN 978-1-894860-46-8

    1. Prayer--Christianity. 2. Prayer--Biblical teaching. I. Title.

BV210.3.M555 2010   248.3'2   C2010-907873-X

For more information on the author please contact:
60 Bristol Road E. Ste, 425
Mississauga, Ontario, Canada
L4Z 3K8
Website www.foundationsministries.org
E-mail praysimply@foundationsministries.org

SPECIAL THANKS

Special thanks to Kathy Bousquet for her invaluable assistance in patiently and diligently editing the original manuscript of this book. Kathy, you made this book writing process such an enjoyable feat.

TABLE
of Contents

THE MODE
— of Prayer

Prayer is humanity's conversation with Almighty God—it is the mortal's mode of communication with the Holy Immortal One.

In the beginning, God walked and talked with Adam and Eve. But due to their disobedience the first sin was committed, a sin that was instigated by Satan. Their sin not only drove them from the Garden of Eden but also broke this original form of fellowship with God (Genesis 3).

God, who has never forsaken His creation and continues to desire relationship with His people, then began to communicate with humanity through various means, such as appearing in some visible form (theophany), e.g., as an angelic being, or speaking to patriarchs, prophets, priests and kings, who would then relay to others the words He had spoken. Throughout the Old Testament we find stories of God communicating with His children and His children communicating with Him.

However, in New Testament times, because of the birth, death and resurrection of Jesus Christ, a new way was made for all people to enter a restored fellowship with God—at least for those who receive Him as their Saviour and Lord.

Therefore, brothers, since we have confidence to enter the Most Holy Place by the blood of Jesus, by a new and living way opened for us through the curtain, that is, his body, and since we have a great priest over the house of God, let us draw near to God with a sincere heart in full assurance of faith, having our hearts sprinkled to cleanse us from a guilty conscience and having our bodies washed with pure water (Hebrews 10:19-22).

Although we no longer experience fellowship with God in exactly the same way as Adam and Eve did, we now have access to God because of Jesus Christ—the Great High Priest. Mankind can once again commune—walk and talk—with God through prayer.

But Satan, our enemy, still continues his strategies, instigating disobedience and sin in order to disrupt our communication with God. Nothing makes Satan more nervous, frustrated and weak than the prayers of God's children. He becomes virtually powerless when we are in conversation with God, and even more so when the conversation is consistent. When we pray from a sincere and a pure heart, Satan and his demons tremble. Why? Because our prayers threaten his kingdom of darkness! When we communicate with God, Satan's strategies are exposed and his powers are broken. He knows that God, who loves to commune with His children, will certainly respond to their voices and release them from his domain of darkness.

Yet we, God's children, neglect this most important and fundamental responsibility—prayer!

We fabricate excuses for avoiding our necessary communication with our Father. We are too busy, too tired, too weak, too messed up, too empty, too hurt, too poor, too confused, too sinful, too distracted—too this and too that!

What a tragedy, since all the excuses by which we have been trapped can be resolved with one act—simply praying! We have complicated what has been designed to be simple for our benefit. Prayer does not benefit God; prayer benefits us, so commune with God in whatever manner you can—pray simply!

When the apostle Paul encouraged us to *"Pray without ceasing"* (1 Thessalonians 5:17, KJV), he had obviously discovered a most beneficial resource and tapped into it—praying continually.

Prayer is not only presented throughout the Scriptures as a required act but is also proven to be fruitful. When we pray, God *"is able to do exceedingly abundantly above all that we ask"* or even dream possible (Ephesians 3:20, KJV). So why not *pray simply—simply pray?*

one

THE ART
—— *of Prayer*

Be Multifaceted: God Loves Variety!

*Lift your eyes and look to the heavens: Who created all
these? He who brings out the starry host one by one,
and calls them each by name. Because of his great power
and mighty strength, not one of them is missing*
(Isaiah 40:26).

Prayer Is an Art

Art is the use of the imagination to create something of
unique and significant beauty. A work of art takes on the
personality of its creator, and as such it is the exclusive
expression of one's individuality.

A number of years ago, I was given an unusual oil
painting as a farewell gift from a place of employment.
This work of art is quite exquisite, and I felt obligated to
display it in a place of prominence—even though it just
does not reflect my individual style or my decor.

In the same manner, we can express ourselves in a
mode of prayer that does not reflect our individuality.
Mistakenly believing that there is a right and wrong way
to pray, we often adopt a prayer style that is contrary to

our personality. But prayer is a work of art! It comes with no prescribed format. Prayer gives expression to what is in the heart and as such should display the personality, style and individuality of the one praying. It should represent who we are, and it should model the beauty and uniqueness of our lives.

The Bible is rife with an array of artistic praying and a variety of praying styles. God loves variety!

Types of Prayers

Here are some biblical expressions of prayer:

Praise: expressing gratitude to Almighty God for His many demonstrated attributes

Worship: reverencing God for His wonders, majestic powers, and dominion over creation

Thanksgiving: acknowledging who God is and what He has done

Request: presenting questions and needs to God and believing for the answers

Petition: lobbying Him for a specific response

Supplication: appealing for answers to the impossible (i.e., when *"heaven [seems like] brass,"* Deuteronomy 28:23, KJV)

Intercession: seeking God's favour or intervention in a life or a specific situation

Prayer: having conversations with God consistently—daily communion

Being Artistic in Prayer

No forms of prayer in the Old and New Testaments were ever rejected by God:

Jehoshaphat praised the Lord before entering battle (2 Chronicles 20).

Abraham worshipped God after each trial (Genesis 17-25).

Moses made his request known in the midst of every situation (Exodus 2-Deuteronomy 34).

David offered thanksgiving in all his battles (1 Samuel 17-1 Kings 2).

Jesus made supplication before going to the cross (Matthew 26:36-45; Mark 14:32-42; Luke 22:39-44; John 17).

The apostles petitioned God when facing opposition (Acts 2-28).

Stephen interceded for his killers (Acts 7:60).

Patriarchs and apostles alike prayed to God at all times, for all things.

Those who needed to communicate with Almighty God did so in the manner that best expressed their feelings and represented their specific needs.

Forms of Artistic Praying

Art in prayer is a creative form that has no fixed definition, whose canvas reflects personality. Follow these biblical examples, envision the canvas, and purpose to copy onto it your own artistic style of communing with God.

Audible Cry

God heard the boy crying, *and the angel of God called to Hagar from heaven and said to her, "What is the matter, Hagar? Do not be afraid; God has heard the boy crying as he lies there"* (Genesis 21:17, emphasis added).

The LORD said, "I have indeed seen the misery of my people in Egypt. **I have heard them crying out** *because of their slave drivers, and I am concerned about their suffering"* (Exodus 3:7, emphasis added).

*They said to Samuel, "**Do not stop crying out to the LORD our God** for us, that he may rescue us from the hand of the Philistines"* (1 Samuel 7:8, emphasis added).

Calling unto God

I am worn out calling for help; *my throat is parched. My eyes fail, looking for my God* (Psalm 69:3, emphasis added).

Then shall ye call upon me, *and ye shall go and pray unto me, and I will hearken unto you* (Jeremiah 29:12, KJV, emphasis added).

Call unto me, and I will answer thee, *and show thee great and mighty things, which thou knowest not* (Jeremiah 33:3, KJV, emphasis added).

Clap unto the Lord

Clap your hands, *all you nations; shout to God with cries of joy* (Psalm 47:1, emphasis added).

"You will go out in joy and be led forth in peace; the mountains and hills will burst into song before you, and all the **trees of the field will clap their hands"** (Isaiah 55:12, emphasis added).

Firmly Positioned

"Do not be afraid. **Stand firm** *and you will see the*

deliverance the LORD will bring you today" (Exodus 14:13, emphasis added).

Therefore put on the full armor of God, so that when the day of evil comes, **you may be able to stand your ground, and after you have done everything, to stand** (Ephesians 6:13, emphasis added).

Kneeling

Come, let us bow down in worship, **let us kneel** *before the LORD our Maker* (Psalm 95:6, emphasis added).

For this reason I kneel *before the Father, from whom his whole family in heaven and on earth derives its name* (Ephesians 3:14-15, emphasis added).

Looking Unto

Look to the LORD *and his strength; seek his face always* (Psalm 105:4, emphasis added).

I will look to see what he will say *to me, and what answer I am to give to this complaint* (Habakkuk 2:1, emphasis added).

Prostrate

When all the people saw this, **they fell prostrate** *and cried, "The LORD—he is God! The LORD—he is God!"* (1 Kings 18:39, emphasis added).

Then David said to the whole assembly, "Praise the LORD your God!" So they all praised the LORD, the God of their fathers; **they bowed low and fell prostrate** *before the LORD and the king* (1 Chronicles 29:20, emphasis added).

Questioning

> **Why, O LORD**, *do you stand far off?* **Why do you hide** *yourself in times of trouble?* (Psalm 10:1, emphasis added).

> *I say to God my Rock, "**Why have you forgotten me? Why must I go about mourning**, oppressed by the enemy?"* (Psalm 42:9, emphasis added).

Reasoning

> *"Come now, **let us reason together**," says the LORD. "Though your sins are like scarlet, they shall be as white as snow; though they are red as crimson, they shall be like wool"* (Isaiah 1:18, emphasis added).

Rejoicing

> *But **may all who seek you rejoice** and be glad in you; may those who love your salvation always say, "Let God be exalted"* (Psalm 70:4, emphasis added).

> *Then Hannah prayed and said: "**My heart rejoices** in the LORD; in the LORD my horn is lifted high. My mouth boasts over my enemies, for I delight in your deliverance"* (1 Samuel 2:1, emphasis added).

Silence

> *"**Be silent, O Israel**, and listen! You have now become the people of the LORD your God"* (Deuteronomy 27:9, emphasis added).

> *Hannah was praying in her heart, and her lips were moving **but her voice was not heard**** (1 Samuel 1:13, emphasis added).

Singing

> *And Mary [sang]: "My soul glorifies the Lord and my spirit rejoices in God my Savior"* (Luke 1:46-47, emphasis added).

> *But I will sing of your strength, in the morning I will sing of your love; for you are my fortress, my refuge in times of trouble* (Psalm 59:16, emphasis added).

Shouting

> *"He prays to God and finds favor with him, he sees God's face and shouts for joy; he is restored by God to his righteous state"* (Job 33:26, emphasis added).

> *We will shout for joy when you are victorious and will lift up our banners in the name of our God. May the LORD grant all your requests* (Psalm 20:5, emphasis added).

Sitting

> *Then King David went in and sat before the LORD, and he said: "Who am I, O Sovereign LORD, and what is my family, that you have brought me this far?"* (2 Samuel 7:18, emphasis added).

> *When I heard these things, I sat down and wept. For some days I mourned and fasted and prayed before the God of heaven* (Nehemiah 1:4, emphasis added).

Standing

> *At that time the Lord set apart the tribe of Levi to carry the Ark of the Lord's Covenant, and to stand before*

the Lord as his ministers, and to pronounce blessings in his name. These are their duties to this day (Deuteronomy 10:8, NLT, emphasis added).

I will stand at my watch and station myself on the ramparts; I will look to see what he will say to me, and what answer I am to give to this complaint (Habakkuk 2:1, emphasis added).

Wailing

You turned my wailing into dancing; you removed my sackcloth and clothed me with joy (Psalm 30:11, emphasis added).

This is what the LORD Almighty says: "Consider now! *Call for the wailing women to come;* send for the most skillful of them" (Jeremiah 9:17, emphasis added).

Whispering

LORD, they came to you in their distress; when you disciplined them, *they could barely whisper a prayer* (Isaiah 26:16, emphasis added).

Be Unique

The art of praying is to recognize the type of prayer needed—the format that will give the greatest expression of communication—and to respond accordingly.

We assume that biblical men and women were experts in praying, yet it is not so. I believe each one lived out his or her own humanity in like manner and in similar situations to those we face today. People related to God in their own artistic manner, and God received their individual expressions by responding according to His will. Their growth and development came from the outflow of heartfelt and earnest prayers to God and from the excitement of seeing how God answered them.

Pray in the posture in which you are most comfortable and feel the most confident. For me this means eyes closed and most often head bowed; that's my personal discipline, enabling me to block out other distractions. However—eyes closed, eyes open, hands raised, sitting, kneeling, bowed low or head raised—pray in whatever posture suits you. Most important are the posture of one's heart and the purposefulness of one's mind. What matters is the reverence expressed as we pray to a Holy God who sits on His throne with angels hallowing His name twenty-four hours a day. Of this one thing we can be assured: God, though He dwells in splendour, gives us the privilege of approaching Him simply and in our own unique style—as long as we come before Him in honour and reverence. *"Therefore, since we are receiving a kingdom that cannot be shaken, let us be thankful, and so worship God acceptably with reverence and awe"* (Hebrews 12:28).

God has created each of us with a unique personality capable of being expressed in prayer without the influence of the styles of those around us. So today, release the artistic expressions of your prayer—by communicating with God in your unique way.

Mix it up a bit—prayer is an art. Be multifaceted!

two

THE ASSET ———— *of Prayer*

Be Rich: God's Resources Are Endless!

> *That in the coming ages he might show the incomparable riches of his grace, expressed in his kindness to us in Christ Jesus* (Ephesians 2:7).

Prayer As an Asset

Probably the worst poverty that can overcome a human being is poverty of the spirit. A person can be poor in material assets but rich in spirit. Likewise a person can be rich in material resources but very poor in spirit.

An asset is something owned or a quality that is of great redeemable value. It is a resource that provides strength and confidence to the owner materially, emotionally or physically. Prayer serves as a vast source of wealth to the owner, as it can bring a benefit far greater than that of any physical commodity.

When we pray, we access our God-given resources in every facet of life. Our Father in heaven, to whom we pray, owns this entire universe: *"The highest heavens belong to the LORD, but the earth he has given to man"* (Psalm 115:16). God has reserved for us vast resources as our inheritance, and His supply can never be exhausted or diminished. Our tool to access these resources is prayer—communication with God.

Prayer is a wonderful asset, as God not only responds to our regular and urgent cries but also has a "bank" of prayers in heaven that works to our benefit. This system is more secure than any earthly bank, and our dutiful, consistent prayers, prayed in righteousness, are stored there on our behalf. Revelation 5:8 tells us that *"each [angel] had a harp and they were holding golden bowls full of incense, which are the prayers of the saints."*

The greatest asset for workers in every occupation is the skilful use of the appropriate tools:

A doctor needs medical equipment.

A carpenter needs the tools of his trade.

A secretary needs pen and paper or a computer.

A driver needs a vehicle.

A preacher needs a Bible.

It stands to reason, therefore, that those who believe in Christ must develop their tool—prayer! The more one engages in prayer, the greater the investment being poured into that heavenly treasury. Prayer is not insurance; prayer is assurance!

Prayer Requires Faith

When we go to the bank for a loan, we may not feel qualified to request the loan, but we do believe the bank has the resources to make that loan possible—that's faith! Prayer requires a practical faith, one that acknowledges the vastness of Jehovah God's treasury and demonstrates personal trust in His ability to dispense it to us.

Our prayers not only access the treasury, but also what Christ Jesus paid for on our behalf and what now by His grace He grants to us freely and abundantly. Ephesians 3:20 declares: *"Now to him who is able to do immeasurably more than all we ask or imagine, according to his power that is at work within us"*—establishing that Christ guarantees resources beyond our wildest imagination.

Through prayer we can access the attributes of God, grow in the characteristics of Christ and experience the power of the Holy Spirit: *"The prayer of a righteous man is powerful and effective"* (James 5:16).

Characteristics, Attributes and Abilities of the Godhead

God the Father is

> omnipotent (all powerful),
> omnipresent (always present),
> omniscient (all knowing),
> sovereign (supreme)
> and holy (pure).

God the Son has power over

> all sickness,
> all natural elements,
> all resources,
> life
> and death.

God the Holy Spirit is able to

> bestow daily provisions,
> provide daily guidance,

impart daily empowerment
and be our Helper at all times.

What an immense treasury from which we can draw!
Through prayer we can access and grow in

the divine nature of God in the area of holiness —
(1 Peter 1:16),
the mission of Christ — (Colossians 2:11-15),
the miracle-working power of Christ — (John 14:12),
the gifts and the empowerment of the Holy Spirit
— (1 Corinthians 12:7-11),
and the fruit of the Spirit — (Galatians 5:22-23), for
a life of godliness.

Prayer as an asset supersedes material wealth.
Solomon said, *"Cast but a glance at riches, and they are gone,
for they will surely sprout wings and fly off to the sky like an
eagle"* (Proverbs 23:5). While wealth is temporary, the
results of prayer are both immediate and eternal. Prayer is
a precious asset whose value never corrodes, never dimin-
ishes and cannot be stolen.

Here's what Jesus says about pursuing eternal investments:

*"Do not be afraid, little flock, for your Father has been
pleased to give you the kingdom. Sell your possessions and
give to the poor. Provide purses for yourselves that will not
wear out, a treasure in heaven that will not be exhausted,
where no thief comes near and no moth destroys. For
where your treasure is, there your heart will be also"*
(Luke 12:32-34).

Prayer Must Be Demonstrated

A number of years ago, I purchased an 18-karat gold

necklace with matching earrings. It was original in design and quite expensive. After boasting about my possessions, I kept them in a safety deposit box for almost a year. Then, after showing the set off to a number of friends, I wore it to a wedding. That same day I lost one of the earrings, and later, before I was able to return it to the safety deposit box, the necklace was stolen. With only one earring left to prove the value of my purchase, I kept it to show friends what I had once owned. But ultimately that became futile. This commodity was no longer worth displaying, as it had lost its value.

Prayer is our most precious asset. We may opt to freely relinquish it but it can never be stolen. It may be temporarily unused but it can never be irreplaceably lost. Consequently, the joy of our relationship with God should drive us to regularly demonstrate the worth of this incredible asset.

The Value of the Asset

Each one of our prayers augments the heavenly treasury from which we can then draw in a time of need. The Bank of Heaven never closes, nor will it ever be devalued or become bankrupt. Deposits and withdrawals can be made at any time, twenty-four hours a day, seven days a week—forever. Unlike using an ATM, we are able to access more than we own and even receive more than requested. The key to accessing the storehouse is in making the request. God simply awaits our appeal for Him to conduct business on our behalf.

Prayer increases in value when we maintain a discipline of regular communication with the Heavenly Banker. We must make wise investments so that we can confidently make regular withdrawals.

Prayer Has Unlimited Potential

The more we pray, the more we accomplish in prayer. The more we pray, the greater the investment. A wise worker stores up resources to draw from at all times.

The wealthiest man who ever lived was King Solomon. Solomon obtained his treasures simply because he prayed and asked God for wisdom. With the gift of wisdom bestowed upon him, his accomplishments were remarkable. We devalue our God-given gifts and blessings when we do not pray. God's desire is to see the greatest good come forth from each of our lives. Our potential riches in Him, gained through prayer, are greater than any stock market can ever achieve—for His glory!

My purpose is that they may be encouraged in heart and united in love, so that they may have the full riches of complete understanding, in order that they may know the mystery of God, namely, Christ, in whom are hidden all the treasures of wisdom and knowledge (Colossians 2:2-3).

You are rich because of Christ—His resources are endless! Prayer yields more than earthly wealth can ever attain. Prayer accesses provision, protection, health, wealth, help, joy, comfort, love, grace, goodness, peace in life, peace over death, wisdom, knowledge, power, hope and so much more.

Be rich in spirit through God's available and endless resources—simply pray!

three

THE ADMINISTRATION —— —— of Prayer

Be Thorough: God Loves Order!

After this manner therefore pray ye: Our Father which art in heaven, Hallowed be thy name. Thy kingdom come, Thy will be done in earth, as it is in heaven. Give us this day our daily bread. And forgive us our debts, as we forgive our debtors. And lead us not into temptation, but deliver us from evil: For thine is the kingdom, and the power, and the glory, for ever. Amen (Matthew 6:9-13, KJV).

Prayer Requires Administration

Administration is the act of managing, controlling or giving structure to a particular function. To pray is to fulfill the mandate of God's Word, which encourages us to communicate with Him and believe that there will be results—that He *will* answer! *"Anyone who comes to him must believe that he exists and that he rewards those who earnestly seek him"* (Hebrews 11:6).

Prayer also carries out God's policies, and wherever policies exist, administration is required. Administrative prayers provide a structure that helps to enhance and increase the capacity of our prayers.

A good administrator does not simply give orders but demonstrates how to accomplish the task. Jesus not only taught about prayer, but His very life was a demonstration of prayer. He gave many examples of administrative praying. These examples were not given as a specific formula but to assist us in covering a broader base, enabling us to be more effective in our endeavour to know and to serve God.

Jesus' All-Encompassing Prayer: John 17:1-26

Jesus prays for His mission (the work of the Lord).
Jesus prays for His followers (all Christians).
Jesus prays for the world (all the unsaved).

Jesus' Intercessory Prayer: Luke 23:34

Jesus prays on mankind's behalf for forgiveness.
Jesus prays on mankind's behalf for salvation.
Jesus shows heartfelt love and compassion for the lost as He pleads to God on their behalf.

When we pray, we begin to

know the heart of God,
grasp the love of Jesus,
understand the direction of the Holy Spirit
and comprehend His Word more fully.

God's burdens are released into our hearts when we pray. Our prayers should not only be for ourselves—which is why administrative praying is of such great importance. Prayer is to be consciously structured so that it encompasses height (God), width (others) and depth (self) as we seek God for current and future needs.

When we pray administratively we learn to encompass the world in our prayers. We will grow in our understanding and relationship with God the Father and begin to sense the heartbeat of Christ His Son.

Administrative praying is inclusive, covering every aspect of the desired outcome.

Variety of Prayers

When the disciples asked Jesus to teach them how to pray He gave them the basis on which to structure their prayers.

The Lord's Prayer

Our Father which art in heaven, Hallowed be thy name. Thy kingdom come, Thy will be done in earth, as it is in heaven. Give us this day our daily bread. And forgive us our debts, as we forgive our debtors. And lead us not into temptation, but deliver us from evil: For thine is the kingdom, and the power, and the glory, for ever. Amen (Matthew 6:9-13, KJV).

Adoration: submitted focus required in prayer

Our Father which art in heaven, Hallowed be thy name. Thy kingdom come, Thy will be done in earth, as it is in heaven.

Praise: to the heavenly Father
Declaration: the kingdom belongs to God
Exaltation: all power belongs to God
Surrender: His will be done

Thanksgiving: for life and blessings

Give us this day our daily bread.

Giving honour to the Great Provider
Giving gratitude for daily provision
Giving thanks for daily protection

Confession: repentance for all sins

Forgive us our debts, as we forgive our debtors.

Forgiveness of sins: both deliberate acts of disobedience and sinful acts committed unknowingly

Supplication: presenting needs to God

And lead us not into temptation, but deliver us from evil.

Heartfelt cries on behalf of others
Request for daily assistance
Request for needed deliverance

Acknowledgement

For thine is the kingdom, and the power, and the glory, for ever. Amen.

Receptivity to God's plan
Relinquishing self to God's purposes
Resting in God's enablement
Acceptance of God's will

Types of Prayer

While He did provide structure, God did not dictate any one mode of prayer to which all creation must submit. Instead, in His wisdom, our Sovereign made the highest form of communication—prayer—a unique, personal and spontaneous act with no limitations.

He gave us the following to assist us in our faith and to give direction as we communicate with Him.

"But when you pray, go into your room, close the door and pray to your Father, who is unseen. Then your Father, who sees what is done in secret, will reward you" (Matthew 6:6).

Praying always with all prayer and supplication in the Spirit (Ephesians 6:18, KJV).

Making Requests: *Therefore I exhort first of all that supplications, prayers, intercessions, and giving of thanks be made for all men* (1 Timothy 2:1, NKJV).

Do not be anxious about anything, but in everything, by prayer and petition, with thanksgiving, present your requests to God (Philippians 4:6).

Giving of Thanks: *Speaking to one another in psalms and hymns and spiritual songs, singing and making melody with your heart to the Lord; always giving thanks for all things in the name of our Lord Jesus Christ to God, even the Father* (Ephesians 5:19-20, NASB).

Meditation: *I remember the days of long ago; I meditate on all your works and consider what your hands have done* (Psalm 143:5).

Intercession: *In the same way the Spirit also helps our weakness; for we do not know how to pray as we should, but the Spirit Himself intercedes for us with groanings too deep for words; and He who searches the hearts knows what the mind of the Spirit is, because He intercedes for the saints according to the will of God* (Romans 8:26-27, NASB).

Approaches to Prayer

There are not only different types of prayer but also different approaches to prayer.

Corporate Prayer: the coming together in agreement of two or more people for a common purpose to

exalt the Lord,
act in repentance,
believe together for the supernatural
or collectively focus on specific needs.

Public Prayer: a time of declaration of the Lordship of Jesus Christ and an act of obedience in the coming together of God's people. Public praying gives opportunity to one person at a time to pray aloud, petitioning God on behalf of the whole. It can also be a time of united declaration—for example, a corporate confession of sin:

> *Therefore the people came to Moses, and said, "**We have sinned**, for we have spoken against the LORD and against you; pray to the LORD that He take away the serpents from us." So Moses prayed for the people* (Numbers 21:7, NKJV, emphasis added).

> *And all the people said to Samuel, "Pray for your servants to the LORD your God, that we may not die; **for we have added to all our sins the evil of asking a king** for ourselves"* (1 Samuel 12:19, NKJV, emphasis added).

Personal Prayer: thanksgiving, supplication and intercession offered at any time and in any place to

seek the Lord,
give thanks,
make our requests known
or intercede on behalf of others.

Devotional Prayer: a personal time set aside for communion with the Lord. This time of speaking to God, listening to Him and then obeying His instructions will

enhance personal faith,
bring preparation and growth
and reveal God's direction for our destiny.

The more we pray, the more we learn how to pray! Praying should never be boring, because the One with whom we are communicating is supremely amazing, wholly powerful, incredibly humorous, exceptionally attentive and infinitely wise.

God loves both freedom and order, and He grants us the privilege of praying to Him in any of the styles He designed. The only requirement, in spontaneity or ritual, is that we pray sincerely—remembering that we are communicating with a Sovereign God.

So pray, with spontaneity from your heart or with scriptural structure—but pray!

four

The Attitude —— of Prayer

Be Humble: God Resists the Proud!

Humble yourselves, therefore, under God's mighty hand, that He may lift you up in due time (1 Peter 5:6).

Attitude of Prayer

Attitude is defined as one's way of thinking and behaving. It is the way in which we regard others and the posture in which we deliberately place ourselves.

When we come before the Lord in prayer, humility is the attitude we must come with. Prayer and pride are opposing forces. When our disposition is one of pride, our prayers are predominantly self-centred and consequently ineffective.

Jesus gave us this illuminating parable:

"Two men went up to the temple to pray, one a Pharisee and the other a tax collector. The Pharisee stood up and prayed about himself: 'God, I thank you that I am not like other men—robbers, evildoers, adulterers—or even like this tax collector. I fast twice a week and give a tenth of all I get.' But the tax collector stood at a distance. He

*would not even look up to heaven, but beat his breast
and said, 'God, have mercy on me, a sinner.' I tell you
that this man, rather than the other, went home justified
before God. For everyone who exalts himself will be
humbled, and he who humbles himself will be exalted"*
(Luke 18:10-14).

When praying, it is important to remember who we are:
*"All the flesh is like grass, and its glory like the flower of grass.
The grass withers, and the flower falls off"* (1 Peter 1:24, NASB,
emphasis added). With this in mind we are more apt to
value Christ for who He is and what He has done for us,
rather than basing our value on who we think we are and
what we have accomplished. The Pharisees were so proud
of their status and their religious knowledge that they
neglected the one essential—the attitude of their hearts.

Humility reminds us that we are sinners. It is only by
His grace that He has chosen to call us His children: *"See
how very much our Father loves us, for he calls us his children,
and that is what we are!"* (1 John 3:1, NLT).

As we focus on God's grace, our heartfelt prayers must
reflect our gratitude for His marvellous love: *"For everyone
has sinned; we all fall short of God's glorious standard. Yet God,
with undeserved kindness, declares that we are righteous. He did
this through Christ Jesus when he freed us from the penalty for
our sins"* (Romans 3:23-24, NLT).

Our accomplishments are meaningless in comparison
to what Christ accomplished on the cross on our behalf.
This is why it is important to always approach God in sincere humility when we pray:

*Your attitude should be the same as that of Christ Jesus:
Who, being in very nature God, did not consider equality*

with God something to be grasped, but made himself nothing, taking the very nature of a servant, being made in human likeness. And being found in appearance as a man, he humbled himself and became obedient to death— even death on a cross! Therefore God exalted him to the highest place and gave him the name that is above every name, that at the name of Jesus every knee should bow, in heaven and on earth and under the earth, and every tongue confess that Jesus Christ is Lord, to the glory of God the Father (Philippians 2:5-11).

Sincerity in our cry to God for mercy demonstrates our dependency on Him, and humility declares our absolute trust in His power.

Two blind men were sitting by the roadside, and when they heard that Jesus was going by, they shouted, "Lord, Son of David, have mercy on us!" The crowd rebuked them and told them to be quiet, but they shouted all the louder, "Lord, Son of David, have mercy on us!" (Matthew 20:30-31).

These men were no longer responding to the dictates of society. They wanted a touch from the Lord, and they were willing to humiliate themselves to get it. Such prayers catch the attention of our God.

This story, however, depicts a different attitude:

As Jesus started on His way, a man ran up to Him and fell on his knees before Him. "Good teacher," he asked, "what must I do to inherit eternal life?"…Jesus looked at him and loved him. "One thing you lack," he said. "Go and sell everything you have and give to the poor, and you will have treasure in heaven. Then come, follow

39

*me." At this the man's face fell. He went away sad,
because he had great wealth* (Mark 10:17-22).

This man's earnest cry for help also caught Jesus' attention, but he was not willing to divest himself of all that was keeping him from humble obedience. Both our actions and our words testify to the true humility of our hearts.

Status does not impress God, and wealth cannot bless God—but humility gets His attention and positions the seeker for His faithful response.

No status in life can guarantee God's mercy. His mercy is neither payment for success nor retribution for failure. It is granted solely because of His loving-kindness. Nothing we do can ever repay Him for His great sacrifice. Our only response must be to humbly submit ourselves before Him, at all times acknowledging His loving-kindness and tender mercies towards us—the children of men.

When we approach God with a right heart attitude, recognizing our desperate need for Him, His ears are open to our prayers. Pray with humility, for God resists the proud!

Posture of Prayer

God declared through Isaiah the prophet that this is the posture that catches God's attention: *"But on this one will I look: On him who is poor and of a contrite spirit, And who trembles at My word"* (Isaiah 66:2, NKJV). One who is contrite shows sincere remorse—sorrow, and a hatred of sin. Humility of spirit is reflected in the very countenance and soul of the person. It is revealed in the heart of one who esteems God highly and esteems others better than self.

Our society exalts those with great gifts and talents but

overlooks a prideful heart. In fact, society generally despises humility and contrition, completely unaware of the New Testament declaration that *"God resists the proud, But gives grace to the humble"* (James 4:6, NKJV). Scripture leaves no room for such erroneous thoughts. David declares that while God dwells in splendour, He does not honour pride: *"Though the LORD is great, he cares for the humble, but he keeps his distance from the proud"* (Psalm 138:6, NLT). Suffice it to say, the proud may pray as much as they desire and as long as they are able to, but God's Word is unchanging. He resists the proud but gives His ear—His attention—to the humble.

The Word of God consistently compels us to approach God in humility. It also instructs us that such humility should never be an act but should be the outflow of our lives, as a daily spiritual adornment: *"All of you, clothe yourselves with humility…Humble yourselves, therefore, under God's mighty hand, that he may lift you up in due time"* (1 Peter 5:5-6). God is pleased with a humble heart—and He responds!

Rewards of Humility

Humility leads to honour: *The fear of the LORD teaches a man wisdom, and humility comes before honor* (Proverbs 15:33).

Humility protects in disastrous times: *Seek the LORD, all you humble of the land, you who do what he commands. Seek righteousness, seek humility; perhaps you will be sheltered on the day of the LORD's anger* (Zephaniah 2:3).

Humility precedes national change: *"If my people, who are called by my name, will humble themselves and pray and seek my face and turn from their wicked ways, then will I hear from heaven and will forgive their sin and will heal their land"* (2 Chronicles 7:14).

Humility brings guidance: *He guides the humble in what is right and teaches them his way* (Psalm 25:9).

Humility results in rewards: *For the LORD takes delight in his people; he crowns the humble with salvation* (Psalm 149:4).

Humility re-establishes the broken: The high and lofty one who lives in eternity, the Holy One, says this: *"I live in the high and holy place with those whose spirits are contrite and humble. I restore the crushed spirit of the humble and revive the courage of those with repentant hearts"* (Isaiah 57:15, NLT).

Humility demonstrates wisdom: *Who is wise and understanding among you? Let him show it by his good life, by deeds done in the humility that comes from wisdom* (James 3:13).

Humility brings favour: That is why Scripture says: *"God opposes the proud but gives grace to the humble"* (James 4:6).

Humility is not weakness; true humility shows great strength. Present yourself in humility of heart before the Holy and Almighty One, and recognize His rewards for such obedience.

I love the saying "Your attitude establishes your altitude." This is absolutely true in prayer; your attitude of humility will establish your altitude with God! *"Humble yourselves, therefore, under God's mighty hand, that he may lift you up in due time"* (1 Peter 5:6).

God guarantees greater heights—be humble!

five

THE ARTICULATION —— —— *of Prayer*

Be Childlike: God Favours Children!

> *"I tell you the truth, unless you change and become like little children, you will never enter the kingdom of heaven"* (Matthew 18:3).

Articulation of Prayer

Articulation is the act of giving utterance or expression. Perfect articulation impresses others but is never needed to impress God—God loves simplicity.

Prayer is not about perfect articulation of a thought or topic. It is not about expressing oneself fluently with elaborate words. Prayer is all about personal, heartfelt communication with our Father.

Adults are often vague in the expression of their needs and desires. Children, on the other hand, verbalize with simplicity: "May I have this?" "I would like that." "When can I get this?" Interestingly, they do so with a resolve in their spirits that the matter is settled. Once they have asked, they simply have to await the objects of their requests.

God cares more about the spirit in which the request is

made than about its clarity of articulation. We may yell or whisper, speak loudly or softly; God is moved not by the mode but by the motive. Jesus responds to childlike expressions that exhibit faith in His ability to perform and fulfill our requests.

Simple Prayers Move Christ

Prayers can be expressed both verbally and non-verbally. Jesus even responded to a silent touch that spoke volumes, indicating to us that God responds to all types of prayer.

A Simple Touch

A woman was there who had been subject to bleeding for twelve years. She had suffered a great deal...When she heard about Jesus, she came up behind him in the crowd and touched his cloak...At once Jesus realized that power had gone out from him (Mark 5:25-30).

A Plea from the Knees

A man with leprosy came to him and begged him on his knees, "If you are willing, you can make me clean." Filled with compassion, Jesus reached out his hand and touched the man (Mark 1:40-41).

An Earnest Petition

Then one of the synagogue rulers, name Jairus, came there. Seeing Jesus, he fell at his feet and pleaded earnestly with him, "My little daughter is dying. Please come and put your hands on her so that she will be healed and live." So Jesus went with him (Mark 5:22-24).

A Desperate Cry

A Canaanite woman from that vicinity came to Him, crying out, "Lord, Son of David, have mercy on me! My daughter is suffering terribly from demon-possession." Jesus did not answer a word. So his disciples came to him and urged him, "Send her away, for she keeps crying out after us"....Then Jesus answered, "Woman, you have great faith! Your request is granted" (Matthew 15:22-28).

Jesus demands no specific format in prayer—He simply hears the cries of His children.

Have you ever heard a child pray with earnestness? I can remember a few I've heard, and each one moved me to tears.

At an orphanage in Thailand, after the worship time, the children were encouraged to pray. It was absolutely thunderous. As they lifted their hands towards heaven, we stood amazed in the presence of God. The intensity of their prayers could be felt despite the language barrier, and we were all convinced, in that moment, that the prayers of these children were being answered.

In Zambia, as I was preparing to preach in a Sunday morning service, the pastor asked for a child to come to the podium and pray blessings on the service. From the children's section a scramble began as many tried to get to the microphone. The first one to respond stirred my heart. She prayed with simplicity, yet with strength and clarity and an obvious trust that God would answer. There were no eloquent words; it was just a simple conversation with God coupled with a faith level that assured us that God would hear and answer. Those prayers still move me. Pray simply!

Simple Prayers Express the Need

Jesus didn't ask for an elaborate speech from those who sought His help. Even though He already knew their need, He asked them to simply articulate it:

> *Then they came to Jericho. As Jesus and his disciples, together with a large crowd, were leaving the city, a blind man, Bartimaeus (that is, the Son of Timaeus), was sitting by the roadside begging. When he heard that it was Jesus of Nazareth, he began to shout, "Jesus, Son of David, have mercy on me!" Many rebuked him and told him to be quiet, but he shouted all the more, "Son of David, have mercy on me!" Jesus stopped and said, "Call him." So they called to the blind man, "Cheer up! On your feet! He's calling you." Throwing his cloak aside, he jumped to his feet and came to Jesus. "What do you want me to do for you?" Jesus asked him. The blind man said, "Rabbi, I want to see"* (Mark 10:46-51).

God requires that we articulate our need or desire.

> *One who was there had been an invalid for thirty-eight years. When Jesus saw him lying there and learned that he had been in this condition for a long time, he asked him, "Do you want to get well?" "Sir," the invalid replied, "I have no one to help me into the pool when the water is stirred. While I am trying to get in, someone else goes down ahead of me." Then Jesus said to him, "Get up! Pick up your mat and walk"* (John 5:5-8).

Simple Articulation Requires Forgiveness

Nothing hinders our ability to communicate with God as much as a lack of forgiveness towards others. When we fail to forgive those who have harmed or wronged us, our prayers are hindered and are perhaps even futile. God's mandate is simply this: He will forgive our debts as we forgive others.

Our hearts respond more freely to God when we do not harbour bitterness against others. Bitterness clouds our thoughts, and unforgiveness hinders our simplicity in praying and our faith in expecting answers.

Children are quick to forgive. One day children are at odds with each other; the next day all is forgiven and they are friends again. We must likewise regularly meet the biblical requirement of forgiveness if we are to approach God wholeheartedly with openness and expectancy: *"Be kind and compassionate to one another, forgiving each other, just as in Christ God forgave you"* (Ephesians 4:32).

Simple Articulation of God's Promises Moves His Hand

As we communicate with God, it is also important to articulate His promises back to Him. Both Old and New Testaments are filled with examples of great men and women of God who quoted the Word of God in their prayers. They articulated what had already been declared to them, using the written Word to express their need.

Whether the Bible is memorized or recited, read aloud or silently, spoken privately or corporately, we can remind God of His great and awesome promises. He is moved by the reminder of them, and He is faithful to keep them!

When children receive promises, they often articulate

them back to remind the one who made them. "Remember what you said? You promised!" Not only do they declare the promise, but they fully expect the one who made the promise to keep it. They may ultimately be disappointed, because men often renege on their promises, but God is not slack concerning His promises towards us—He is faithful to them (2 Peter 3:9). His Word reminds us *"For all the promises of God in Him are Yes, and in Him Amen"* (2 Corinthians 1:20, NKJV). *"Abraham never wavered in believing God's promise. In fact, his faith grew stronger, and in this he brought glory to God. He was fully convinced that God is able to do whatever he promises"* (Romans 4:20-21, NLT).

God loves to commune with His children. He is not limited to an earthly mode of communication, but He chose this method of prayer for our benefit. He never intended that this be complicated but that it would be a simple articulation of our hearts. He said,

> *"Ask and it will be given to you; seek and you will find; knock and the door will be opened to you. For everyone who asks receives; he who seeks finds; and to him who knocks, the door will be opened...If you, then, though you are evil, know how to give good gifts to your children, how much more will your Father in heaven give good gifts to those who ask him!"* (Matthew 7:7-11).

When you pray—pray as a child. God loves and responds to such simplicity!

six

THE ANGUISH
of Prayer

Be Faithful: God Never Forsakes His Own!

"My God, my God, why have you forsaken me?" (Mark 15:34).

God Is Faithful in Times of Anguish

Anguish is an excruciating state of suffering, pain, distress and sorrow. Although God's intent was to bless His creation forever, the life of bliss He intended for us is now filled with toil and pain because of man's original fall into sin and disobedience.

There are times in life when we are overwhelmed with despair and discouragement. Often, even though our prayers have intensified for a specific situation, heaven is silent and God seems so very far away. Anguished prayer becomes a reality as we struggle to find the inner strength to push beyond this point of despair. Even when our knees become sore, our minds and spirits are exhausted, and no answer seems close at hand, praying through to victory must be our resolve.

The Bible reminds us that though God may be silent, He is definitely not distant. He is present with us, enabling us to endure the situation at hand until the timing for His perfected answer is fulfilled. Our God promises to reward those who diligently seek Him (Hebrews 11:6). His plan for mankind is to grant to all "hope and a future" (Jeremiah 29:11).

God has not forgotten nor forsaken us: *"Can a mother forget the baby at her breast and have no compassion on the child she has borne? Though she may forget, I will not forget you!"* (Isaiah 49:15). So it is imperative that we not waver from this mandate: *"Pray without ceasing"* (1 Thessalonians 5:17, KJV), through every dark moment we may encounter.

Prayerfully Endure Anguish

The greatest example God gave us of His unforgettable love and presence was in His Son. Jesus suffered immensely to demonstrate to us that God has every intention of enabling us to overcome. There were times when heaven was silent for the divine Son of God, and only afterwards could the perfected will of God in all the anguish He endured be seen. His agony on the cross depicts the deepest feelings of separation from His Father: *"And at the ninth hour Jesus cried out in a loud voice, 'Eloi, Eloi, lama sabachthani?' which means, 'My God, my God, why have you forsaken me?'"* (Mark 15:34). Jesus felt what we feel in our times of despair. Yet God's Word cannot lie—He promises to never leave or forsake His own (Hebrews 13:5). The psalmist, David, declared, *"Even though I walk through the valley of the shadow of death, I will fear no evil, for you are with me"* (Psalm 23:4).

Jesus also demonstrated how to overcome the temptations and tactics of the enemy (Matthew 4:1-10) so that we, too, could be assured of victory. All that He endured assures us that He fully comprehends and empathizes with the severity of our trials. For reasons that may only be revealed at the end of time, God allows us to go through anguish even as we continue in heartfelt communication with Him.

In our seasons of seemingly endless trials, we must never give up in the face of adversity. The time will come when God's grace, strength, peace, joy and, yes, victory will personally be extended. In the most difficult times of life, press on in prayer. Remember that Christ despaired while attempting to fulfill God's plan. He suffered, just as many today are suffering—yet He overcame!

Great Sufferers—Mighty Overcomers

David, a man after God's heart and one of the most victorious warriors in the Word of God, wrote about his frequent times of despair. He recognized that God makes the rain to fall on the just and the unjust (Matthew 5:45) and that He allows all of humanity to experience, at varied times in life, every conceivable emotion. Yet David's psalms teach us that while we exist in pain or feel separated from God, we must continue to communicate with Him openly and honestly:

Why are you in despair, O my soul? And why have you become disturbed within me? Hope in God, for I shall again praise Him For the help of His presence (Psalm 42:5, NASB).

Answer me when I call to you, O my righteous God. Give me relief from my distress; be merciful to me and hear my prayer (Psalm 4:1).

I call on you, O God, for you will answer me; give ear to me and hear my prayer (Psalm 17:6-8).

David was often in the depths of anguish, yet he laboured and prayed in faith. He never doubted God's ability to perform His wonders or His power to transform the situation he was facing. Sometimes the purpose for David's anguish was immediately revealed. At other times, it was hidden, the answer delayed. But David didn't cease to pray, and neither should we. We don't know which situations God will choose to answer immediately and which ones later—so continue praying in anguish, just as David did:

Hear my voice when I call, O LORD; be merciful to me and answer me. My heart says of you, "Seek his face!" Your face, LORD, I will seek. Do not hide your face from me, do not turn your servant away in anger; you have been my helper. Do not reject me or forsake me, O God my Savior. Though my father and mother forsake me, the LORD will receive me (Psalm 27:7-10).

Hear, O LORD, and answer me, for I am poor and needy. Guard my life, for I am devoted to you. You are my God; save your servant who trusts in you. Have mercy on me, O Lord, for I call to you all day long. Bring joy to your servant, for to you, O Lord, I lift up my soul. You are forgiving and good, O Lord, abounding in love to all who call to you (Psalm 86:1-5).

Whatever pain, trial, anguish or sorrow you are faced with today, pray along with David, for he is one of the proofs that God hears and God will answer: "*Show the wonder of your great love, you who save by your right hand those who take refuge in you from their foes. Keep me as the apple of your eye; hide me in the shadow of your wings"* (Psalm 17:7-8). Make David's resolve yours today—Lord, I trust You; hear my prayer!

Divine Answers in Anguish

There are many New Testament examples of those who endured hardship and yet overcame. Some, like Stephen, endured hardship for the sake of generations to come yet died without seeing the answer themselves. Saul, who witnessed Stephen's death, saw immediately the answer to his prayers.

> *But Stephen, full of the Holy Spirit, looked up to heaven and saw the glory of God, and Jesus standing at the right hand of God. "Look," he said, "I see heaven open and the Son of Man standing at the right hand of God." At this they covered their ears and, yelling at the top of their voices, they all rushed at him, dragged him out of the city and began to stone him. Meanwhile, the witnesses laid their clothes at the feet of a young man named Saul. While they were stoning him, Stephen prayed, "Lord Jesus, receive my spirit." Then he fell on his knees and cried out, "Lord, do not hold this sin against them." When he had said this, he fell asleep* (Acts 7:55-60).

Even in death, Stephen's prayer could not be silenced. And though he didn't realize it, his passion outlived him and his fervency convicted men. Saul stood there watching, and later, perhaps even because of Stephen's intercession, he was forgiven by God. *"And when the blood of your martyr Stephen was shed, I stood there giving my approval and guarding the clothes of those who were killing him"* (Acts 22:20). Now transformed, he became Paul—one of the greatest New Testament apostles. Only God knows the purpose of our trials and the timing of His answers, so press on in faithful prayer!

Why is Stephen's anguished prayer so relevant to us? Because it is a reminder that even in death we are more than conquerors through Jesus Christ our Lord (Romans 8:37)! God did not forget Stephen.

We cannot fathom God's purposes for the future. But one day all things will be unveiled before us, and we will understand and appreciate His marvellous wonders.

Surrendering in Prayer

Jesus, in the Garden of Gethsemane, struggled with the silence of heaven. Yet He trusted that God had a greater plan and surrendered to His will. He pleaded, *"My Father, if it is possible, may this cup be taken from me. Yet not as I will, but as you will"* (Matthew 26:39). May that be our resolve and our cry in times of despair, that God's ultimate purpose would prevail and that His will would overrule ours. Surrendering fully to God when things just do not make sense is not easy. It's during those times that we must rest in the knowledge of His all-encompassing love, continue to pray expectantly and never give up—for God does not forsake His own!

This book was birthed during a season of anguish in my own life. At the very time when the ministry to which God had called me was finally experiencing great break-throughs, I was afflicted. I struggled for almost two years with throat polyps, which became hardened nodules. In the season of great blessings, I was advised to undergo throat surgery. This was distressing, as I felt an evangelist without a voice is of no use to God, and the doctor's prognosis was quite negative.

Hoping that God would perform an instant miracle, I agonized in prayer night and day. Yet there was no change. In fact, in the ensuing weeks, as I continued with my speaking engagements, the condition worsened. Finally, I underwent the surgery. I experienced all the pain and the anguished trauma of healing. It was in that season, however, that God birthed this book in my spirit. I could not speak for months and had no choice but to learn to pray without speaking, worship without the company of others and trust God for His restoring power and for His purpose to be fulfilled.

Now, years later, I can look back and see His purpose. He led me into a new level of prayer, teaching me how to pray! The rich communication that I experienced with God while I could not speak has enabled me to see my God in a number of new lights. Fame, status, money or power could not have enriched my life as that season of distress did. Those anguished prayers significantly impacted the ministry to which God has called me to be faithful, and the remembrance of that time is forever sealed into my spirit.

The anguish of prayer is real! When God seems so far away, continue praying fervently, for He cannot forget His beloved child. You are the apple of His eye and His rare and precious jewel. You will be kept as pure gold: *"He knows the way that I take; when he has tested me, I will come forth as gold"* (Job 23:10).

Be faithful. Pray always—even in anguish.
God never gives up, and neither should we!

seven

THE ANCHOR
— of Prayer

Be Confident: God Assures Stability!

We have this hope as an anchor for the soul, firm and secure. It enters the inner sanctuary behind the curtain, where Jesus, who went before us, has entered on our behalf (Hebrews 6:19-20).

The Anchor—Our Hope

An anchor is a heavy device lowered from a ship to grip the bottom of the sea. The anchor affixes itself securely and gives stability.

Our anchor is the hope we have in Jesus Christ and in His finished work. We can rest assured that we have everlasting security in Jesus, as He is unmovable, unshakeable and unbreakable, holding us securely in all situations. We can simply rest in Him, placing all our weight upon Him and trusting Him in every situation we face. When we communicate with God in prayer, we activate the hope that holds us steadfast in Christ Jesus.

An anchor brings security in the most tumultuous of times, but it doesn't prevent the storm. Therefore, when we pray we activate our trust, our hope, in the one who can bring us through the ferocious storm safely. Through prayer we develop the inner security of knowing that, whatever happens, Christ Jesus has both us and the situation firmly in His grip.

Throughout the Bible, there are many examples of those who have proven the strength and power of this great anchor of hope.

Securely Anchored in Tumultuous Times

As Defender

Moses rested his hope in the knowledge of his Defender whenever opposition raged against him. He learned how to stand in the midst of all the situations he faced as he endeavoured to lead Israel:

> *Then Moses cried out to the LORD, "What should I do with these people? They are ready to stone me!" The LORD said to Moses, "Walk out in front of the people. Take your staff, the one you used when you struck the water of the Nile, and call some of the elders of Israel to join you. I will stand before you on the rock at Mount Sinai. Strike the rock, and water will come gushing out. Then the people will be able to drink." So Moses struck the rock as he was told, and water gushed out as the elders looked on* (Exodus 17:4-6, NLT).

As Redeemer

Job was stripped of everything—property, possessions, family and health. Yet Job leaned on the Redeemer of all mankind, knowing that when life no longer made sense he could trust in Him. Even as his body decayed before his eyes, Job's hope was secure in the One who would bring him through the tragedies and torments. In the end, God restored Job's losses with more blessings than ever before.

> *"But as for me, I know that my Redeemer lives, and he will stand upon the earth at last. And after my body has decayed, yet in my body I will see God! I will see him for myself. Yes, I will see him with my own eyes. I am overwhelmed at the thought!"* (Job 19:25-27, NLT).

As Provider

The widow of Zarephath believed in the power of prayer, and she put her hope in the only one who could provide for her when all else was gone. Her cupboards were empty, creditors were at the door and her family was in absolute despair, yet she leaned on the great Provider and found that He held her securely in the palm of His hands, turning the tide around on her behalf:

> *One day the widow of a member of the group of prophets came to Elisha and cried out, "My husband who served you is dead, and you know how he feared the LORD. But now a creditor has come, threatening to take my two sons as slaves"* (2 Kings 4:1, NLT).

As Rebuilder

Nehemiah put his hope in the Rebuilder who restored broken and destitute people and even rebuilt their nations. Nehemiah was in the midst of an impossible situation that moved him to remind God of His promises. He knew that the Word of God consistently tells us that we have this hope in the One who goes before us and who makes our way perfect. He took comfort in that and saw hope lived out once again through the success he was given in spite of great opposition.

> *"The people you rescued by your great power and strong hand are your servants. O Lord, please hear my prayer! Listen to the prayers of those of us who delight in honoring you. Please grant me success today by making the king favorable to me. Put it into his heart to be kind to me"* (Nehemiah 1:10-11, NLT).

As Protector

When the Hebrews were up against those who despised God's people, Esther fasted and prayed in hope to the Protector. This young woman recognized that God protects those who boldly live out His will. Inside the palace she was alone, but she anchored her hope in the One who grants peace and inner security and who entered the room with her as she appealed to the king for the plight of a nation:

> *Then Esther sent this reply to Mordecai: "Go and gather together all the Jews of Susa and fast for me. Do not eat or drink for three days, night or day. My maids and I will do the same. And then, though it is against the law, I will go in to see the king. If I must die, I must die"* (Esther 4:15-16, NLT).

As Deliverer

Hezekiah appealed in faith to the Deliverer who was able fight his battles against the enemy. Other kings had given in under such great threats, but Hezekiah sent for a prophet who sought God's Word on behalf of the king and his people. They found hope as a sure anchor to hold them steady in the midst of a threatening situation. Hezekiah knew that though they were outnumbered by the enemy, the One who promised to hold His children securely in the palm of His hand would deliver them from the strongest of forces:

> They told him, "This is what King Hezekiah says: Today is a day of trouble, insults, and disgrace. It is like when a child is ready to be born, but the mother has no strength to deliver the baby. But perhaps the LORD your God has heard the Assyrian chief of staff, sent by the king to defy the living God, and will punish him for his words. Oh, pray for those of us who are left!" (2 Kings 19:3-4, NLT).

As Adjudicator

David prayed in hope, morning and night, to the Judicious One who grants justice in His own time. After years of running from Saul, and later even from his own son, David learned that God is a righteous judge, a God of justice in treacherous times:

> Then Saul said, "I have sinned. Come back, David my son. Because you considered my life precious today, I will not try to harm you again. Surely I have acted like a fool and have erred greatly." "Here is the king's spear," David answered. "Let one of your young men come over and get it. The LORD rewards every man for his righteousness and faithfulness. The LORD delivered you into my hands today, but I would not lay a hand on the LORD's anointed. As surely as I valued your life today, so may the LORD value my life and deliver me from all trouble" (1 Samuel 26:21-24).

As Faithful One

Daniel faced opposition many times during his time in the Babylonian kingdom, yet he always remained calm and continued praying in the assurance that the Faithful One would not leave him in a time of trouble. So strong was his hope in God's grip that he even slept in peace in the midst of lions:

> Now when Daniel learned that the decree [against praying to any god or man but King Darius] had been published, he went home to his upstairs room where the windows opened toward Jerusalem. Three times a day he got down on his knees and prayed, giving thanks to his God, just as he had done before. Then these men went as a group and found Daniel praying and asking God for help (Daniel 6:10-11).

As the Empowering One

Peter raised his voice in hope to the Empowering One who gives courage to tackle difficult situations:

> When they saw the courage of Peter and John and realized that they were unschooled, ordinary men, they were astonished and they took note that these men had been with Jesus. But since they could see the man who had been healed standing there with them, there was nothing they could say (Acts 4:13-14).

Victory through the Anchor of Hope

A familiar saying states "Prayer moves the hand of God." Likewise we can say, "Prayer moves the Anchor into position." When we put our trust in the one who holds all things securely in His hands, we can be sure that even though the storm rages on, we will not be shipwrecked. Prayer assures us we can have God's presence, peace and rest in the midst of all of life's circumstances.

I have experienced multiple miracles in my lifetime when, through prayer, my anchor of hope was firmly fixed on Christ. Here are just a few:

Defender: I was unjustly accused by peers, which brought despair and despondency, yet God turned it all around and worked it out for greater good.

Redeemer: I suffered the loss of some relationships and close friendships and was stripped of financial security, yet God has made the latter blessings greater than the former.

Provider: I have spent many years of doing the work of an evangelist, and God has faithfully provided for all my needs, even in seasons of financial difficulties.

Rebuilder: Ministering in war-ravaged African countries such as Congo and Liberia, I arrived after the devastation of wars, yet sensed the absolute direction of God and saw Him use our frailties to remind these broken nations of how they can find hope in the plans He has for their people.

Protector: I raced out of a town in Southern Congo, having been warned of God just minutes before martial law was imposed. I was warned of God in Northern India that danger was ahead as our vehicle came upon a Hindu celebration, where an attempt was made to overturn our van.

Deliverer: I have been under every form of spiritual attack from the enemy, yet walked in the peace of God, which enabled us to envision future changes in the international borders and boundaries that were currently restricting His children from working together in unity.

Adjudicator: I had my passport stolen in a third world country as the passport official lied, saying that he had not touched it, yet God caused someone else to mysteriously bring it forward.

Faithful One: I've seen signs, miracles and wonders performed in other peoples' lives, year after year, as I minister in the frailty of this body, and I also recognize God's touch upon my own life and ministry.

Empowering One: I've received His divine touch and inspiration to minister to people of varying cultures, languages and tribes, in small and large churches, to cold, hot and lukewarm hearts.

God assures us of victory in every situation, especially when our anchor is in position before the storm even hits.

Perhaps you could write your own chapter about all that God has done on your behalf. The very recollection of this firm anchor grants peace and rest when we are in the midst of the storms of life.

Activate your hope today through the anchor of prayer, trusting that even if you fail, *"Christ Jesus, who died—more than that, who was raised to life—is at the right hand of God and is also interceding for us"* (Romans 8:34).

Fix the anchor of your hope in God—
He assures His stability!

eight

THE AUTHORITY
of Prayer

Be Bold: God's Power in You Is Amazing!

For in Christ all the fullness of the Deity lives in bodily form, and you have been given fullness in Christ, who is the head over every power and authority (Colossians 2:9-10).

Authority is the delegated power that gives a person the right to enforce obedience. It is personal influence arising from one's position.

In prayer, authority can be coupled with ardency. *Ardency*, this twin of authority, means to be passionate. To be ardent is to enthusiastically and zealously pursue something with keen interest and confidence. Spiritually, it means to pray with passion and expectation, in the knowledge that our prayers will bring about change. Praying ardently with authority captivates our bodies, souls, minds and spirits because of the forthrightness of the prayers.

Authoritative Prayers

Only when we fully comprehend who has delegated

His authority to us and who assigns us to act on His behalf will we begin to know the power we have to influence people and overcome the enemy. The devil cowers in fear when God's children walk in their delegated authority. Satan knows that the position given to us is one of might and power, because it is the same power in which Jesus operated and the same power that rested on the apostles, as demonstrated in the book of Acts.

The Old Testament records numerous examples of authoritative prayers prior to the New Testament revelation of Jesus Christ and the declaration of how God's power can work in us. These stories are of men and women who understood their God-given authority and who prayed ardently in situations requiring great boldness.

Abraham and His God

> Then the LORD said, "Shall I hide from Abraham what I am about to do?"...The men turned away and went toward Sodom, but Abraham remained standing before the LORD. Then Abraham approached him and said: "Will you sweep away the righteous with the wicked? What if there are fifty righteous people in the city? Will you really sweep it away and not spare the place for the sake of the fifty righteous people in it?" (Genesis 18:17-24).

Abraham stood in determination before the Lord as he interceded for his family. The Lord relented, and Abraham's nephew, Lot, was spared.

When we understand the authority that has been delegated to us, we will persist in intercession, believing that God will act in response and expecting that our prayers will lead to victory.

Moses in Crisis

Moses answered the people, "Do not be afraid. Stand firm and you will see the deliverance the LORD will bring you today. The Egyptians you see today you will never see again. The LORD will fight for you; you need only to be still" (Exodus 14:13-14).

Moses stood with persistence and petitioned God for a specific need during a great time of crisis. God heard his request and sent the answer immediately (Exodus 14:15-31). Throughout the book of Exodus there are numerous accounts of Moses calling out to God in the time of need. Later, Joshua followed in his footsteps.

Moses' Bold Declaration

But Moses sought the favor of the LORD his God. "O LORD," he said, "why should your anger burn against your people, whom you brought out of Egypt with great power and a mighty hand?" (Exodus 32:11).

"Oh, what a great sin these people have committed! They have made themselves gods of gold. But now, please forgive their sins—but if not, then blot me out of the book you have written" (Exodus 32:31-32).

Again, Moses stood before God, pleading to the Lord to alter His plan. This conversation depicts his full understanding of the authority he had been given to present such petitions to his Creator. Moses feared God but also ardently held God to His Word.

Joshua and the Enemy

So Joshua marched up from Gilgal with his entire army,

including all the best fighting men. The LORD said to Joshua, "Do not be afraid of them; I have given them into your hand. Not one of them will be able to withstand you."...On the day the LORD gave the Amorites over to Israel, Joshua said to the LORD in the presence of Israel: "O sun, stand still over Gibeon, O moon, over the Valley of Aijalon." So the sun stood still, and the moon stopped, till the nation avenged itself on its enemies, as it is written in the Book of Jashar. The sun stopped in the middle of the sky and delayed going down about a full day (Joshua 10:7-13).

Future generations should be able to learn from and build upon our passionate exploits. Joshua had observed Moses and learned from his boldness before God. He took his stand and authoritatively gave a command to the sun and the moon. God heard him and responded with great power (v.14).

Elijah's Keenness

Elijah's ardency in prayer is cited in the New Testament as an example for believers to follow: *"The prayer of a righteous man is powerful and effective. Elijah was a man just like us. He prayed earnestly that it would not rain, and it did not rain on the land for three and a half years"* (James 5:16-17).

James uses Elijah's strong and insistent prayer to remind us of the power of ardent prayers. Elijah's prayer when he was facing the prophets of Baal contained a mere sixty words, yet it brought down fire from heaven. Elijah had learned such authority in prayer through the many miracles that had preceded this one. *Our* mighty miracles will be preceded by us faithfully stepping into and acknowledging even the smallest of miracles. We cannot run before we learn to walk. We learn to believe God for the small things so that we will confidently anticipate His answers in the larger arenas of life.

At the time of sacrifice, the prophet Elijah stepped forward and prayed: "O LORD, God of Abraham, Isaac and Israel, let it be known today that you are God in Israel and that I am your servant and have done all these things at your command. Answer me, O LORD; answer me, so these people will know that you, O LORD, are God, and that you are turning their hearts back again." Then the fire of the LORD fell and burned up the sacrifice, the wood, the stones and the soil, and also licked up the water in the trench. When all the people saw this, they fell prostrate and cried, "The LORD—he is God! The LORD—he is God!" (1 Kings 18:36-39).

God affords us marvellous privileges that can lead us into enormous authority. We must know how to stand righteously before God and determine to ardently petition Him until He responds on our behalf and for His glory.

Elisha's Bold Request

Although Elijah was a mighty man of God and was passionate in his function as a prophet, Elisha, his understudy, anticipated even greater miracles. Elisha caught Elijah's passion and demanded a double portion of his anointing in order to operate in the same office of the prophet:

When they had crossed, Elijah said to Elisha, "Tell me, what can I do for you before I am taken from you?" "Let me inherit a double portion of your spirit," Elisha replied. "You have asked a difficult thing," Elijah said, "yet if you see me when I am taken from you, it will be yours—otherwise not" (2 Kings 2:9-10).

Many other examples of ardency and authority exist in the Word of God. Let's conclude with one New Testament example.

Peter and John's Passion

On their release, Peter and John went back to their own people and reported all that the chief priests and elders had said to them. When they heard this, they raised their voices together in prayer to God. "Sovereign Lord," they said, "you made the heaven and the earth and the sea, and everything in them" (Acts 4:23-24).

Peter and John, who had been jailed and beaten, immediately went back to their people to report on the audacity of the unbelievers. With a God-lit fire in their souls, they began to demonstrate in prayer that they would not cower in the face of adversity and neither would they relent in their task of proclaiming the Good News. Passion in prayer brings results. Their passion was contagious; the people became enveloped in the fervour of such ardent prayers.

"Now, Lord, consider their threats and enable your servants to speak your word with great boldness. Stretch out your hand to heal and perform miraculous signs and wonders through the name of your holy servant Jesus." After they prayed, the place where they were meeting was shaken. And they were all filled with the Holy Spirit and spoke the word of God boldly (Acts 4:29-31).

Praying with authority and ardency are particularly dear to my heart, as I have proven time and time again the absolute power that rests with us as children of God. I have travelled numerous Third World countries spanning southern, eastern and western Africa. I have ministered in Asia, from Sri Lanka and Indonesia to India and Cambodia. The life lessons I have learned are appropriate to every country: God has given us power to oppose the works of darkness and call people into His marvellous light. He has given us authority to rescue those captured by the enemy, regardless of how intense the opposition is. Whether it was in Indonesia with Islamic threats, or in India where defiant Hindus attempted to thwart the work of God, or in Congo with intensified spiritual warfare by mediums, or in Zambia with witchcraft opposition or even in Liberia with political uncertainties, God wrought victories at all times.

The Word of God gives us this profound and proven declaration:

> For though we live in the world, we do not wage war as the world does. The weapons we fight with are not the weapons of the world. On the contrary, they have divine power to demolish strongholds. We demolish arguments and every pretension that sets itself up against the knowledge of God, and we take captive every thought to make it obedient to Christ (2 Corinthians 10:3-5).

God's power is awesome! We can pray both ardently and authoritatively, knowing that as we do the strongholds of the enemy will be destroyed and God's work will be accomplished.

Our God-Given Authority

Because of what Jesus accomplished on the cross, our position in Christ grants us unprecedented boldness. We have authority because of the new covenant that Jesus secured for us. In and through the power of His Holy Spirit, we can recognize and walk in the spiritual authority Christ has secured on our behalf.

> *For what was glorious has no glory now in comparison with the surpassing glory. And if what was fading away came with glory, how much greater is the glory of that which lasts! Therefore, since we have such a hope, we are very bold. We are not like Moses, who would put a veil over his face to keep the Israelites from gazing at it while the radiance was fading away* (2 Corinthians 3:10-13).

We have scarcely apprehended the full measure of Christ's power—deposited in us for His glory and for the building up of His kingdom!

**So pray simply, but be bold—
passionately pursue your God-given authority.**

THE ADMONISHMENT —— —— *of Prayer*

Be Strong: God Has No Capacity to Be Weak!

Be strong in the Lord and in his mighty power. Put on the full armor of God so that you can take your stand against the devil's schemes (Ephesians 6:10-11).

To admonish is to urge or to reprimand. We are urged to know the grace of God and to also know our position in Christ, standing firmly in the liberties His death and resurrection have afforded us. To only partially accept Christ's finished work on the cross is to deny the power of the godhead over our lives and to assume an attitude of defeat. Being *"strong in the Lord and in his mighty power"* necessitates a resolute faith when we pray.

Even before the incarnation of Christ, God urged His people to depend on the support system His strength and power provides. He admonished Joshua, *"Be strong and courageous. Do not be terrified; do not be discouraged, for the LORD your God will be with you wherever you go"* (Joshua 1:9).

As we wholeheartedly acknowledge the true source of our power and strength, we will learn to communicate

73

with God in dependence on His provision of all we need to overcome defeat.

Admonishment in Prayer

God doesn't know weakness: *"Who is this King of glory? The LORD strong and mighty, the LORD mighty in battle"* (Psalm 24:8). We are to abide in the strength and exist in the power of this Mighty One. As we pray through various situations, we will, at times, be in a weakened state. We can, however, pull down strongholds through the provision of God's strength. Focusing on our weakness can lead us into defeat; but when we are focused on God's strength, even our weakness becomes a catalyst for victories.

> *To keep me from becoming conceited because of these surpassingly great revelations, there was given me a thorn in my flesh, a messenger of Satan, to torment me. Three times I pleaded with the Lord to take it away from me. But he said to me, "My grace is sufficient for you, for my power is made perfect in weakness." Therefore **I will boast all the more gladly about my weaknesses, so that Christ's power may rest on me*** (2 Corinthians 12:7-9, emphasis added).

Jehovah God admonishes us to be strong because of who He is, despite who we are and how we feel.

Admonished to Act

Look at the ones who, though they perceived themselves to be weak, were used by God in intense battles in the past. As they placed their hope in His ability to act, each one of them was victorious over his enemies.

Moses

> Then the LORD said to Moses, "Why are you crying out to me? Tell the Israelites to move on. Raise your staff and stretch out your hand over the sea to divide the water so that the Israelites can go through the sea on dry ground" (Exodus 14:15-16).

Moses' job was to be the conduit used by God for signs and wonders for the people to see. In fear, Moses cried out to God, who, in turn, admonished him to simply and confidently obey His instructions. *"Then Moses stretched out his hand over the sea, and all that night **the LORD drove the sea back** with a strong east wind and turned it into dry land. The waters were divided"* (Exodus 14:21, emphasis added).

Moses obeyed, and God brought the victory. God commands us to step out in the strength that we have. Our actions are merely the earthly representation of God's heavenly response to our prayers and petitions.

Joshua

> *"Then Joshua fell facedown to the ground in reverence, and asked him, '**What message does my Lord have for his servant?**'"* (Joshua 5:14, emphasis added). God simply expects us to communicate with Him so that He can convey his instructions to us. As we fulfill them, God acts. His mission prevails, and all take note that it is God who accomplished such a great task.

> Now Jericho was tightly shut up because of the Israelites. No one went out and no one came in. Then the LORD said to Joshua, "See, I have delivered Jericho into your hands, along with its king and its fighting

*men. March around the city once with all the armed
men. Do this for six days"* (Joshua 6:1-3).

We are admonished to be vigilant in our demonstration of strength in the Lord's work. Joshua was merely human, just as we are, yet God put him in the most difficult situations. He did not send him alone, however; nor did He expect him to accomplish the impossible by his own power. God had the impossible covered; Joshua was to simply be obedient—seek God's direction, obey His answers and then march boldly before the enemy in demonstration of His might and power.

*"When the trumpets sounded, the people shouted, and at the
sound of the trumpet, when the people gave a loud shout, the
wall collapsed; so every man charged straight in, and they took
the city"* (Joshua 6:20). God simply seeks willing vessels who first acknowledge that only God's power can bring changes in nations, governments, people, situations and circumstances and who will then willingly submit to His agenda, even in their weakness.

Gideon

*"But sir," Gideon replied, "if the LORD is with us, why
has all this happened to us? Where are all his wonders
that our fathers told us about when they said, 'Did not
the LORD bring us up out of Egypt?' But now the
LORD has abandoned us and put us into the hand of
Midian." The LORD turned to him and said, "**Go in
the strength you have** and save Israel out of Midian's
hand. **Am I not sending you**?"* (Judges 6:13-14,
emphasis added).

Whatever God promises He will accomplish! When we

pray, then, we must move from the position of seeing victory as a probability and move into our assured position of expectancy. My admonishment in prayer is this: ask God for His direction, challenge God for His involvement and then trust God for His victory!

Fearless Strength

In 2008—seven years after God had granted me the vision for it—we conducted the first-ever women's leadership conference in Zambia. Women from eleven nations of Southern Africa were invited. The conference was designed to equip women in their leadership roles so that they could return to their own countries and mentor other women into leadership.

During the two years of planning, countless battles were waged against us. There were financial impossibilities. The emotional challenges became overwhelming, as many rose up in opposition against the conference. It took its toll physically as a lack of sleep became a tremendous factor.

Then during the week of the conference there were many unexpected upheavals that threatened to cancel it. The president of the country died the day before the conference commenced, necessitating a time of national mourning. One of the dormitories burned down, the women just barely escaping with their lives. There were many financial constraints, undue financial expectations and excessive border-crossing dilemmas for women coming into Zambia from other countries.

Yet, in weakness, fear and trembling we stormed heaven for God's strength to continue on. And we saw Him, in His mighty power, begin to turn every scenario around. We saw His handprint everywhere. God had instructed; we were obedient. He overruled every battle and wrought seemingly inconceivable victories. By the end of the conference, one major phrase was coined about the week: "We have been positioned in this place, at this time, with all these warriors, for 'such a time as this'!"

We all recognized that this was not an earthly agenda but a heavenly mission, in which we obeyed and God acted. We made ourselves available to declare His sovereignty over all those nations. He used simple women of faith and prayer—weak, yet strong in Him—to accomplish significant tasks. The admonishment again is, Be strong, for God is with us!

The Weapons of our Warfare

We often desire elaborate answers for simple questions while ignoring the admonition already given. David, in 1 Samuel 17, refused to adorn himself in earthly armour because he saw how ineffective it would be against a giant twice his size. He knew that only as we clothe ourselves in the full armour God has prescribed, through the working of His power and strength, will strongholds be demolished.

Put on the full armor of God so that you can take your stand against the devil's schemes. For our struggle is not against flesh and blood, but against the rulers, against the authorities, against the powers of this dark world and against the spiritual forces of evil in the heavenly realms. Therefore put on the full armor of God, so that when the day of evil comes, you may be able to stand your ground, and after you have done everything, to stand. Stand firm then, with the belt of truth buckled around your waist, with the breastplate of righteousness in place, and with your feet fitted with the readiness that comes from the gospel of peace. In addition to all this, take up the shield of faith, with which you can extinguish all the flaming arrows of the evil one. Take the helmet of salvation and the sword of the Spirit, which is the word of God. **And pray in the Spirit on all occasions with all kinds of prayers and requests.** *With this in mind, be alert and always keep on praying for all the saints* (Ephesians 6:11-18, emphasis added).

To be strong in the power of the Lord also requires a level of fearlessness. The apostles were in the minority in the days after Jesus' death, but in every situation they faced they learned to trust God and walk in His miracles. They demonstrated His strength and power in the face of impossibilities:

The crowd joined in the attack against Paul and Silas, and the magistrates ordered them to be stripped and beaten. After they had been severely flogged, they were thrown into prison, and the jailer was commanded to guard them carefully. Upon receiving such orders, he put them in the inner cell and fastened their feet in the stocks. **About midnight Paul and Silas were praying and singing hymns to God,** *and the other prisoners were listening to them. Suddenly there was such a violent earthquake that the foundations of the prison were shaken. At once all the prison doors flew open, and everybody's chains came loose* (Acts 16:22-26, emphasis added).

Admonished to Pray

The same God who urged the patriarchs, prophets and apostles to relate to Him in prayer during times of great need offers us the same admonishment.

Seek Him

I love those who love me, and those who seek me find me (Proverbs 8:17).

"You will seek me and find me when you seek me with all your heart" (Jeremiah 29:13).

Call unto Him

He will call upon me, and I will answer him; I will be with him in trouble, I will deliver him and honor him (Psalm 91:15).

The LORD is near to all who call on him, to all who call on him in truth (Psalm 145:18).

Trust Him

"As for God, His way is perfect; The word of the LORD is proven; He is a shield to all who trust in Him" (2 Samuel 22:31, NKJV).

Trust in the LORD with all your heart and lean not on your own understanding (Proverbs 3:5).

Personal Admonishment

My encouragement to you is the apostle Paul's prayer:

*For this reason **I kneel before the Father, from whom his whole family in heaven and on earth derives its*** *name. I pray that out of his glorious riches he may* *strengthen **you** with **power** **through** his **Spirit** **in*** *your **inner** **being*** (Ephesians 3:14-16, emphasis added).

My admonition to you is what Scripture declares to every believer:

Be strong in the Lord and in his mighty power (Ephesians 6:10).

Pray in the Spirit on all occasions with all kinds of prayers and requests (Ephesians 6:18).

The Spirit helps us in our weakness. We do not know what we ought to pray for, but the Spirit himself inter-cedes for us with groans that words cannot express (Romans 8:26).

Remember: God has no capacity to be weak!

So, as you obey, allow God's strength to be made perfect in your weakness— and simply pray!

ten

THE ANCESTRY ——
—— *of Prayer*

Be Reminded: God Communes with His Children!

> *For you did not receive a spirit that makes you a slave again to fear, but you received the Spirit of sonship. And by Him we cry, "Abba, Father." The Spirit himself testifies with our spirit that we are God's children* (Romans 8:15-16).

Ancestry—Our Right to Commune with God

Ancestry is our inherited line. While we may change many things in our lives, we cannot change our ancestry. Our DNA—the nucleic acids that form the molecular basis of heredity in our personal family tree—is permanent and is passed on from one generation to another.

The history of prayer is similar. Prayer was birthed with God in the Garden of Eden where He first communed with His children, our ancestors Adam and Eve. When we are born again we become His sons and daughters and we inherit His blueprint for our lives. Prayer—communication with our Father—becomes a permanent aspect of our spiritual DNA!

Then the man and his wife heard the sound of the LORD God as he was walking in the garden in the cool of the day...The LORD God called to the man, "Where are you?" (Genesis 3:8-9).

God's intent has always been to have communication with His children, and one of Satan's strategies from the beginning has been to keep us from personally interacting with Him. Our enemy will convince us not to pray, frustrate us as we attempt to pray, and discourage us by hindering our prayers. He does whatever it takes to block the communication lines. However, his efforts are futile when a child of God determines to utter even one word to the Father. The moment we begin to pray, the lines of communication are automatically opened. We have God's attention immediately, and His mercies are extended towards us, His easily ensnared children.

Our Ancestors Communed with God

The word *commune* means "to communicate," that is, to converse, connect with and convey thoughts to. Prayer is not only speaking to God but also taking time to wait upon Him, listening to Him, hearing His voice in our spirits and responding to what we have heard.

Our ancestors recognized the extensiveness of prayer, which encompasses so much more than simply making demands. They modelled for us, in their own unique way, their interaction with God.

Enoch Walked with God

And after he became the father of Methuselah, Enoch walked with God 300 years and had other sons and daughters. Altogether, Enoch lived 365 years. Enoch walked with God; then he was no more, because God took him away (Genesis 5:22-24).

One can only imagine what walking with God for those many years entailed! Certainly in that time, Enoch must have talked to God, connected with God, conveyed his thoughts to God and listened as God conveyed His thoughts to him. One can only imagine the conversations they held with each other until the day God determined to take Enoch away to be with Him forever. This type of communion reminds us of God's original intent back in the Garden of Eden with Adam and Eve.

Enoch's journey would have been quite difficult, considering the ungodly era in which he lived. The Bible does not tell us that there were others who served Jehovah wholeheartedly in those days, so it seems Enoch had very few godly examples around him. Yet, he must have maintained a constant communion and dialogue with God, because his life is recorded as one that was a pleasure to Him (Hebrews 11:5).

Abraham Fell on His Face Before God

God appeared to Abraham and spoke personally to him throughout his life's journey:

*When Abram was ninety-nine years old, **the LORD appeared to him and said**, "I am God Almighty; walk before me and be blameless. I will confirm my covenant between me and you and will greatly increase your numbers." **Abram fell facedown** (Genesis 17:1-3, emphasis added).*

Hagar Heard the Voice of God

> *The angel of the LORD found Hagar near a spring in the desert...She gave this name to **the LORD who spoke to her**: "You are the God who sees me," for she said, "I have now seen the One who sees me"* (Genesis 16:7-13, emphasis added).

It is evident that those who have gone before us interacted frequently with God. The conversations God and Moses had together typified their close relationship. Perhaps we have made prayer so dismal and boring that we have lost the kind of rich communication our Almighty Father desires.

Heart to Heart Communication

God Spoke to Moses

> ***God** also **said** to Moses, **"I am the LORD. I appeared to** Abraham, to Isaac and to Jacob as God Almighty"* (Exodus 6:2-3, emphasis added).

> ***The LORD called** to Moses **and spoke to him** from the Tent of Meeting* (Leviticus 1:1, emphasis added).

> ***And the LORD said** to Moses, "I will do the very thing you have asked, because I am pleased with you and I know you by name"* (Exodus 33:17, emphasis added).

Moses Spoke to God

> *The people came to Moses and said, "We sinned when we spoke against the LORD and against you. Pray that the LORD will take the snakes away from us." So*

Moses prayed for the people (Numbers 21:7, emphasis added).

Moses said to the LORD, *"You have been telling me, 'Lead these people,' but you have not let me know whom you will send with me. You have said, 'I know you by name and you have found favor with me.' If you are pleased with me, teach me your ways so I may know you and continue to find favor with you. Remember that this nation is your people." The LORD replied, "My Presence will go with you, and I will give you rest"* (Exodus 33:12-14, emphasis added).

The Bible is full of such conversations between God and man, and each one demonstrates to us the simplicity God desires in His relationship with His children.

Our Ancestral Heritage

Upon our acceptance of the Lord Jesus Christ as our Saviour, we became a part of His family line. We have been grafted in, by the shed blood of Jesus.

But some of these branches from Abraham's tree—some of the people of Israel—have been broken off. And you Gentiles, who were branches from a wild olive tree, have been grafted in. So now you also receive the blessing God has promised Abraham and his children, sharing in the rich nourishment from the root of God's special olive tree (Romans 11:17, NLT).

And if the people of Israel turn from their unbelief, they will be grafted in again, for God has the power to graft them back into the tree (Romans 11:23, NLT).

Irrevocable Covenant

The covenant God made with us is irrevocable. As His people, our lineage is secure:

> *"This is the covenant I will make with the house of Israel after that time, declares the Lord.* **I will put my laws in their minds and write them on their hearts.** *I will be their God and they will be my people. No longer will a man teach his neighbor, or a man his brother, saying, 'Know the Lord'; because they will all know me, from the least of them to the greatest. For I will forgive their wickedness and will remember their sins no more"* (Hebrews 8:10-12, emphasis added).

Becoming a part of Christ's family is a personal choice—it is the only opportunity we have to freely choose our ancestry! Paul declares in his epistle to the Romans that salvation comes to us freely because of the love and grace of God, giving us the opportunity to be transformed by the power of God into His likeness and be grafted into His spiritual family lineage. As we acknowledge our ancestral line, we must also walk confidently in the assurance that what God has done in the past, He will likewise do for us and through us today—and even more so! *"I tell you the truth, anyone who has faith in me will do what I have been doing. He will do even greater things than these, because I am going to the Father"* (John 14:12).

Faith activates the miraculous. Prayer, however, activates faith and gives the assurance to walk in or exercise what faith has declared. When we commune with God, we gain insight about how to execute the things He has sanctioned.

A word used frequently by the patriarchs and by God Himself throughout the Scriptures is *remember!* Remember that our ancestors were able to make it through all that they faced because of His mighty power. God has a proven track record!

David declares in confidence:

> *I will utter hidden things, things from of old—what we have heard and known, what our fathers have told us. We will not hide them from their children; we will tell the next generation the praiseworthy deeds of the LORD, his power, and wonders he has done* (Psalm 78:2-4).

The covenant God made with Abraham has also been extended to us, revealing the extent of our family heritage and our God-ordained purposes. Our hearts should be truly grateful for our ancestors' victories and our inherited privileges!

We can gladly boast in God's power and be assured that when we pray to our Father—at all times, for all things, in all circumstances—He will listen! He will not only listen, but He will also respond (speak to us) as we open our hearts, minds and spirits to commune with Him. *"Ask and it will be given to you; seek and you will find; knock and the door will be opened to you. For everyone who asks receives; he who seeks finds; and to him who knocks, the door will be opened"* (Matthew 7:7-8).

What a heritage we can boast of! Our God is known as the Alpha and Omega—the Beginning and End (Revelation 21:6). He is the one who gave us life and rightfully owns us. He guided our forefathers all the days of their lives, and He has promised to do the same for us.

Remember that we have a great cloud of witnesses (Hebrews 12:1)—people we can emulate who have proven God's love and power and have also proven that mere humans can communicate with Almighty God.

Some of our ancestors were fearful, yet they engaged in formidable exploits with God. Some of them were faith-filled as they prayed; others prayed with little faith, which then grew to mighty faith as they witnessed and were a part of God's answers.

Simple People—Faith-Filled Prayers

Guidance: Abraham's servant prayed for guidance when he was sent by his master to another country to find a wife for Isaac. He uttered these words: *"Oh LORD, God of my master Abraham, give me success today"* (Genesis 24:12) and found the answer already waiting for him as he arrived in that foreign land.

Direction: Manoah (Samson's father) prayed for direction after God told his wife that she would give birth to a special son. *"O LORD, I beg you, let the man of God you sent to us come again to teach us how to bring up the boy who is to be born"* (Judges 13:8). God did hear Manoah's request and gave them the instructions they had requested.

Desperation: Hannah, having reached the end of her rope in her season of barrenness, sought God with great determination. *"In bitterness of soul Hannah wept much and prayed to the LORD. And she made a vow, saying, 'O LORD Almighty, if you will only look upon your servant's misery and remember me, and not forget your servant but give her a son, then I will give him to the LORD for all the days of his life'"* (1 Samuel 1:10-11). God heeded her request and gave her a son, Samuel, who became one of Israel's great leaders.

Dedication: Solomon, commissioned by God to build the temple, prayed heartfelt words of adoration to God as he dedicated to Him the works of his hands. *"May your eyes be open toward this temple day and night, this place of which you said you would put your Name there. May you hear the prayer your servant prays toward this place"* (2 Chronicles 6:20). God responded to Solomon's prayers and visited both Solomon and the congregation of Israel with His glorious presence.

Repentance: Nehemiah repented for the sin of an entire nation. *"I confess the sins we Israelites, including myself and my father's house, have committed against you"* (Nehemiah 1:6). God heard Nehemiah and made provisions for Israel to be restored.

Deliverance: The apostles, who had been imprisoned and were then threatened upon their release, knew only one course of action—prayer. They sought God for his intervention on their behalf: *"Now, Lord, consider their threats…Stretch out your hand to heal and perform miracles signs and wonders through the name of your holy servant Jesus"* (Acts 4:29-30). God answered in His supernaturally marvellous manner: *"After they prayed, the place where they were meeting was shaken. And they were all filled with the Holy Spirit and spoke the word of God boldly"* (Acts 4:31).

We are enriched by the words and deeds of our ancestors who have demonstrated to us God's willingness to personally interact with His children! They have shown us that communication with our Father is the blending of voices—our voices to His ears, and His voice to our hearts.

Remember the ancestry of prayer. What God has recorded in His Word is to serve as a constant reminder to us of what we can accomplish today. God used simple people to fulfill His supernatural plans then, and God desires to use simple people now.

As God's children, walking in a spiritual heritage, we have been given the keys to His Kingdom to conduct His works. Our ability to continue this rich heritage is gained in only one way: by communing with God—through *prayer!*

**Walk in the confidence of these memories today.
We have an inherited privilege: communication
with Abba Father. Simply pray!**

PRACTISE MAKES PERFECT
—— Prayer: Pass or Fail?

I struggled with certain subjects during my academic years. In grade school it was mathematics, in high school it was calculus, in university it was economics, and in Bible college my "thorn in the flesh" was Greek. Yet in each setting there were teachers who encouraged me to persevere. One teacher in particular declared emphatically, "If you work on this daily, I guarantee it will become easier than you ever dreamed possible." I listened, and although this was a subject I did not like and thought impossible to master, I ultimately obtained an excellent grade.

Similarly, many of us struggle with this subject called "prayer." Prayer requires effort, dedication and daily practice. The joy of this subject is that there never has been, nor will there ever be, an exam! Our Great Teacher—Jesus— knowing how much His students struggle with prayer, even took it upon Himself to stand at the right hand of God and intercede on our behalf, so that as we pray in earnest, our prayers are already covered by His prayer. *"Christ Jesus, who died—more than that, who was raised to life—is at the right hand of God and is also **interceding** for us"* (Romans 8:34, emphasis added).

He brings our requests before Almighty God, who aligns them with His eternal purpose, which ultimately is that all might be saved. *"Therefore He is also able to save to the uttermost those who come to God through Him, since He always lives to make intercession for them"* (Hebrews 7:25, NKJV).

The rewards of prayer are significant and incredible—significant, because we are guaranteed answers for just simply trying, and incredible, because prayer is not motivated by fear of failure—it is heart-driven! Each student is given the opportunity to simply make an expression of prayer from the heart, in any capacity or manner. And, because of the effort, a passing grade is automatically guaranteed. Through the simplicity of prayer, the lives of all who call upon God can be blessed and enriched, in good times and bad—and prayer will continue to advance the student into higher realms with God.

This book is not a guidebook. It is intended to provoke my fellow students to ever greater heights in prayer. All that is required is to make the best effort we can in response to a faithful, loving and kind Teacher—our Lord and Saviour, Jesus Christ.

Practice makes perfect. Prayer—the highest form of communication with God—can only serve to enhance our lives. I urge you to daily practise prayer, taking time to record not only your prayers but also the answers to them. You will be amazed to discover just how consistently and how marvelously He responds!

Since the benefits of praying are overwhelming and there really is no failing grade, pray simply and simply pray—you're guaranteed to pass!

You Can Do It! ———

Start today by adding your own simple words to this model of prayer given to us by Jesus. He taught this to His disciples, not as a mantra for rote recitation, but as a guideline for a personal prayer life.

The Lord's Prayer (Matthew 6:9–13, NKJV)

"Our Father in heaven"

Awesome God; Creator of the Universe; our God and friend; Abba, Holy and faithful Father; Supreme God; our King; our Lord, our Master, our Shepherd, our rock, strength, peace, hope; our Messiah and Great Redeemer.

"Hallowed be Your name"

Your name is higher than every other name, the name that delivers, saves, heals, sets free; guides, restores, protects, defends. You are the Bread of Life, Lion of the Tribe of Judah, Wonderful Counsellor, Lamb of God. Your Name alone is mighty—Jehovah, Shepherd and King; Saviour; Everlasting God; Immanuel; King of Kings.

"Your kingdom come"

Only You know the past, the present and the future. Lead us into Your plans; let Your presence come and dwell among us here on earth; let Your supreme rule take over our lives and our nation. You are the Head of the Church, the great High Priest. Rule and reign over all that we attempt to do—let Your kingdom be established.

"Your will be done On earth as it is in heaven"

Teach us what to do, what to say, how to pray, how to live. We want to fulfill Your plans and Your purposes; we want to walk in Your counsel, live in righteousness, exist in purity, abide in love and give out Your love to others; we want to be prepared for all that You have for our lives. Show us what to do; help us to live out Your plan, to think right, behave right and treat others right.

"Give us this day our daily bread"

Thank You, Lord, for the daily provisions with which You have blessed us. Help us to be grateful for Your daily blessings. We thank You for Your great kindness in the plenty You have given, and we present to You our need for the lack that we are facing. Your mercies never cease; great is Your faithfulness; Your mercies begin afresh each morning. Like the psalmist David, we give thanks to You, Lord, for You are good! For Your mercy endures forever. Bless us again today, O Lord! You know our needs, and You know our wants and desires. We remind You of them today. Grant only the ones that are best for us, and thank you in advance for tomorrow's promises!

"And forgive us our debts"

Father, we have all sinned and fallen short of Your glory. But because of Your great love, forgive us our sins today. Forgive us for the sins we have knowingly committed and the sins we unconsciously entered into. Our unconfessed sins are always before You, so we confess them today and thank You for Your forgiveness. Have mercy on us, O God, because of Your unfailing love. Because of Your great compassion, blot out the stain of our sins. Grant us earnest hearts that we might not sin against You.

"As we forgive our debtors"

Father, as You have forgiven us, so we forgive others. We forgive those who have wronged us, hurt us, abused us, mistreated us, cheated us. Help us to forgive them over and over until the pain departs from our spirits. Heal the wounds that are left and give us compassion for the ones who have so wronged us. We honour your Word in which Solomon declared that *"A good name is more desirable than great riches; to be esteemed is better than silver or gold"* (Proverbs 22:1). Teach us to live by Your Word, and enable us to forgive up to seventy times seven.

"And do not lead us into temptation"

Master, please protect us from the temptations in this life. Teach us to be content with what you have given us, keep us from yearning after material prosperity, and move us to seek first Your kingdom. Protect us from desires that will destroy our lives' purposes; shield us from temptations that will hinder Your presence from overshadowing our lives. Protect us from unhealthy desires; help us not to be captivated by the sins of the flesh (greed, anger, jealousy, quest for power, self glory). Lord, like Solomon (Proverbs 30:8-9) we ask, "Give us neither too much nor too little; for when we are too full, we can get independent, saying, 'Who needs God?' And when we are too poor, we might steal and dishonour the name of our God." Keep us from the tempter's snares.

"But deliver us from the evil one"

Lord, Satan desires to destroy our lives; he knows our weaknesses and our faults—he has seen them in action. Shield us from this evil one. Set Your holy guard around us so that our faults will not overtake us; help us as we step away from the evil things Satan plants before our eyes. Embed your Word in our spirits so that we will not sin against you. Keep us from the subtle traps of the enemy. Our hearts belong to You, Lord. We seal our commitment to You; deliver us with Your righteous hand. You are our Advocate.

"For Yours is the kingdom"

This nation is Yours; our families, both secular and sacred, are Yours; our whole being belongs to You. Do as You wish, Lord; direct us in the path that You have ordained for our lives. Lead us into Your kingdom plans. We declare Your Lordship over this country, this city, our families, our friends and ourselves. Lord, take charge of everything that pertains to us in both life and godliness.

"and the power and the glory"

You are most powerful, God, glorious in all Your ways. Your name is to be praised; You are our mighty deliverer, strong tower, refuge and strength. You are peace, hope and light. You are our joy and victory. We honour Your name and glorify Your being, Most High God. There is no one like You—holy, righteous, powerful, sovereign and just. You are our everything. We bless You because You are God and there is none like You!

"forever. Amen"

Thank you, God, for being with us yesterday, for being here for us today, and for being the one guaranteed to be there tomorrow. Praise the Lord, and amen—so let our prayers be heard. Lord, hear and answer our prayers!

Pray simply and simply pray!

THE ART OF PRAYER
I Can Be Multi-Faceted

THE ASSET OF PRAYER
I Am Rich

THE ADMINISTRATION OF PRAYER
I Will Be Thorough

THE ATTITUDE OF PRAYER
I Will Be Humble

THE ARTICULATION OF PRAYER
I Can Be Child-Like

THE ANGUISH OF PRAYER
I Will Be Faithful

THE ANCHOR OF PRAYER
I Will Be Confident

THE AUTHORITY OF PRAYER
I Will Be Bold

THE ADMONISHMENT OF PRAYER
I Will Be Strong

THE ANCESTRY OF PRAYER
I Am Reminded